I Thought So—

~: VOLUME 2 :~

I Thought So—

∽: VOLUME 2 :∽

More Original Epigrams

Michael Lipsey

LOST
COAST
PRESS

Lost Coast Press
155 Cypress Street
Fort Bragg, CA 95437
(800) 773-7782
www.cypresshouse.com

Cover and book design by
Michael Brechner / Cypress House
Photo of the author by Mindy Pines

LIBRARY OF CONGRESS CATALOGING-IN-PUBLICATION DATA

Lipsey, Michael, 1941-
    I thought so-- : a book of epigrams / Michael Lipsey. -- Fort
Bragg, CA : Lost Coast Press, c2008-
    v. ; cm.
    ISBN: 978-1-882897-94-0 (v. 1) ; 978-1-935448-03-7 (v. 2)
Vol. 2 has subtitle: More original epigrams.
Includes bibliographical references.
    1. Epigrams. I. Title.
PS3612.I67 I25 2008   2007030526
                        811/.6--dc22

PRINTED IN THE USA
2 4 6 8 9 7 5 3 1

FSC
Mixed Sources
Product group from well-managed
forests and other controlled sources

Cert no. SW-COC-002283
www.fsc.org
© 1996 Forest Stewardship Council

~:~

If, as they say, I am only an ignorant man trying to be a philosopher, then that may be what a philosopher is.
— Diogenes

~:~

I want to depart this life with honorable steel piercing my heart and a piercing epigram on my lips.
— Edmond Rostand (*Cyrano de Bergerac*)

~:~

Anyone can tell the truth, but only a very few of us can make epigrams.
— W. Somerset Maugham

~:~

Wearing out seven number two pencils is a good day's work.
— Hemingway

~:~

∽:∽

This book is dedicated to the great conversation that continues through the ages. To Diogenes, Zeno, Confucius, Epictetus, Cicero, Ecclesiastes, Buddha, Rinzai, Maimonides, Rumi, Shakespeare, Samuel Johnson, Pope, La Rochefoucauld, Pascal, Blake, Voltaire, Rabelais, Emerson, Thoreau, Kafka, Nietzsche, Schopenhauer, Mark Twain, Wilde, Shaw, Dickinson, Mencken, Stein, Einstein, Wittgenstein, Artaud, Orwell, McLuhan, Burroughs, M. L. King, Dylan, Singer, Thurber, Dr. Seuss, and a hundred others whose words fill the vast room. I sit quietly on a stool in the farthest corner, listening, and finally dare to put in a word or two. Forgive my chutzpah.

Contents

CONTENTS

~:~

I THOUGHT SO—

VOLUME 2

~:~

AFTER MY FIRST BOOK of original epigrams was published, I spent a lot of time answering the question: What is an epigram? This was unexpected because I had begun *I Thought So — A Book of Epigrams* by defining the epigram. But who would read the introduction to a book of epigrams? Presumably one just opens it and begins reading here and there. And I am grateful to all my readers, whether they skip around, dip in, stroll, or methodically plod through every word I have deposited on these pages, including this introduction. Without readers I could not join the 3,000-year-old conversation begun by thinkers like Diogenes and Confucius.

In starting out to write a book of epigrams, it is a given that everything about life, manners, and human nature has already been said by wiser heads during three millennia of inscribing and scribbling. For example, I wrote:

> *Only a small percentage are insane —*
> *but a large percentage are always on the edge.*

And I recently discovered that 2,300 years ago Diogenes said:

> *Most men are within a finger's breadth of being mad.*

But in my last book I said:

> *Crazy people are only a little crazier.*

And so the conversation goes. Would you like to join in? The room has no walls, no clocks, and an infinite number of chairs around the seminar table.

Circumstances change, such as the avalanche of technology in our time, but human nature remains the great constant. We're as vain and foolish as our ancestors of eighty generations back. Where we are wise, we are wise in the ways that they were wise. Greedy or generous, optimistic or pessimistic, chaste or lecherous, truthful or mendacious, brave or cowardly, quick-tongued or tongue-tied, funny, sarcastic, intuitive, credulous, envious, inventive, ambitious — human nature is the great constant.

True originality is nearly impossible for the epigrammatist, and yet the field remains open to a close observer of the endless shadings of human behavior and of this splendid world. I follow a well-worn path through the forest, but the trees have millions of leaves, and the sunlight reflected from those leaves changes every moment.

The raw material is the bedrock of human nature. The fleeting expression that tells what is really going on, the slight that still stings forty years later, the falling in love, the furies, the generous lifelong friendships, the back stab, the front stab, the liars, and those who would die before they would tell a lie. Whether you are watching the news, chatting with your spouse over the Sunday papers, in a tense meeting at work, visiting a friend in the hospital, stopping for a drink on the way home, kicking down doors in Baghdad, or at your first day of kindergarten, human nature is on display and in play. You get on, and get along in this world, not by trying to change human nature, which would be like trying to demolish a wall with your head, but by empathy and understanding and epigrams.

The epigram is condensed human nature, a quick way of telling a long story, a snapshot instead of a panorama, a miniature, not a mural. It gets right to the point because it is the moral of the tale, the hard lesson learned. You have just a line or two, a dozen words or two. To an epigrammatist a sonnet is an epic poem.

Suppose yourself an epigrammatist—and if you have read this far, you could be one. You saw something that made you realize something last night. And you got it down, but it took a paragraph. Interesting for your journal, or the novel you're planning to write, but to carve it down to an epigram, to make this balloon take flight, will require some verbal weight loss.

You climb into the basket, the ropes are loosened, but the balloon does not ascend. Some ballast must be jettisoned. First to go overboard are the adverbs. What use is an epigram if it needs a *usually* or an *obviously?* This gets us off the ground, but not above the trees. Unload the adjectives! This is about the truth—who cares if it's brick red or lime green, obese or emaciated, pockmarked, bodacious, lovable or nefandous?

The first principle of an epigrammatist was stated best by William Strunk Jr. and E. B. White in *The Elements of Style*. "Omit unnecessary words!" The gist must be carved out of the verbiage. Basic gist recipe: take one noun, add one verb.

> *See everything for the first time.*
> — Saith Me

See the word, the word is *everything*. And you are seeing this word for the world for the first time. And you can see it for the first time a million times because the word represents the infiniteness of everything that can be seen. Or see it in this simile—everything is like something else:

> *Uttering a word is like striking a note*
> *on the keyboard of the imagination.*
> — Ludwig Wittgenstein

We respect the power of the word—even God speaks to us one word at a time. In the beginning was the word. What's the word? Will you put in a good word for me? Are you serious? Word! You have my word on it. A man of his word. The last word on it. Amen.

We begin with the word—and now (as we perfect a cold glass of gin with a bit of lemon peel) we need to add the twist:

> *It is not possible to enumerate all the kinds of vanity.*
> — La Rochefoucauld

Rendered into *anglais* in eleven words. No adjectives, no modifiers—just the gist of it, period. Enumerating is counting, but this is the uncountable, like the stars in the sky. La Rochefoucauld had the thought, the realization; he saw the light reflected off the leaf. And the confidence not of "It is difficult to…" but "It is not possible to…" The confidence of a duke who led his ferocious knights into many battles. His balloon rose again and again. No one has come up with anything better in the 300 years since he wrote it. I sit at his feet. He put in the twist—but as everything has already been said, the epigrammatist does not hope for originality:

> *Vanity of vanities, saith the Preacher,*
> *vanity of vanities; all is vanity.*

La Rochefoucauld was morose. He believed that life is a matter of appearances, of simulation, of putting up a front, of putting on your game face. Which is reasonable considering that he was in and out of favor with the capricious French court. The Preacher was also morose— some of the early rabbis wanted to delete Ecclesiates from the Bible because they thought him pessimistic, pleasure seeking, and cynical. Perhaps even an Epicurean.

> *Nothing prevents us from being natural*
> *so much as the desire to appear so.*
> — La Rochefoucauld

The only advantage I have over La Rochefoucauld is the pure dumb luck of being an English speaker in America, at a time when, for better or worse, we are at the center of the world's gaze. While Martial may have been the big cheese of epigrammatists, he wrote in Latin, still spoken widely in Vatican City. English has become the first world language, the Esperanto Esperanto never became. The Russians and the French and the Chinese hate this, but they study English if they are ambitious. Being a native speaker of English, especially the American variety, is a muscular leg up. They may loathe us in Iran, but they're watching our TV programs. Serbians write a lot of good epigrams, but even their Balkan neighbors don't care to hear them.

I write in Midwestern mid-twentieth-century American English. That is my mother tongue, but not my mother's mother tongue. My language might be inflected by a childhood in which one side of the family chatted in Yiddish and the other in Hungarian. Maybe a slight note from being raised in the home of my grandmother, who grew up in Whitechapel, where the Queen's English was mutilated into cockney. Queen Victoria gave my great-grandfather a shiny cartwheel penny in the park. He spent it. Later he sailed to Canada, snuck across the US border (undocumented worker or illegal alien?), and went to work in a sweatshop to raise the funds to import the rest of his brood to Chicago. The house of my grandmother was actually his house, and he occupied the front stoop, studying *The Forward* through coke-bottle lenses plus a magnifying glass. And ignoring the talkative drunks from the corner bar and the alms-begging students from the nearby yeshiva.

Chicago has the best American English for terse directness. Asked about some corruption, Alderman Paddy Bauler, who ran the 43rd ward from his saloon, replied, "Chicago ain't ready for reform." Mayor Richard J. Daley was asked his opinion on a report and he said, "What the hell do the experts know?" The motto of Chicago was "I Will!" until Mike Royko changed it to "Where's Mine?" Here are a few other classic Chicagoisms:

Abner Mikva decided to volunteer in a Democratic campaign. He walked into the local committeeman's office and was immediately asked: "Who sent you?" Mikva replied, "Nobody sent me." And the retort came back from the cigar-chomping pol: "Well, we don't want nobody that nobody sent."

Boss Jake Arvey was asked why he picked Adlai Stevenson to run for governor: "To perfume the ticket."

Growing up by the elevated tracks you wonder if the people in the passing trains looking at you wonder what it would be like to live by the elevated tracks. And you can walk down the alley to the station on the corner, put a dime in the turnstile, and be in the magical Loop in a few minutes. Fifty years later and 2,000 miles away, I can still hear the clatter of the train, and the screech as it stopped at the corner. All summer long we sat on the upstairs back porch, at eye level with the passengers, spitting watermelon seeds over the railing, and exclaiming when an interurban train came by, on its way to someplace unimaginably far away, like Elgin, inhabited by Germans making clocks. My grandmother would always say that one day she was going to go to the corner, climb those stairs, get on the interurban, and ride it to wherever it went.

At twenty-six I migrated to California, the State of Mind. From the endless rows of lettuce in the central valley to the endless movies now emanating from Hollywood, it is not a place known for brevity. Minnesota would have been linguistically preferable, but it would be hard to write when your fingers are frozen for half the year. Forty years in California and I am not quite the complete Californian: I still talk fast, assume all politicians are on the take (aren't they?), toss off value judgments, and remain unaware of my breath except when I am out of it.

I seesaw between writing and art, sometimes going from my office to my studio several times a day. Writing epigrams is 90 percent thinking, 1 percent writing, and 39 percent rewriting. Like trying to make two plus two equal five. I have as much luck driving as I do sitting here trying to write. When lightning strikes, some are finished in seconds. But many come very slowly, crawling out of the ocean and growing rudimentary legs on which they follow me about, insisting that they are not evolutionary dead ends.

Stage 1 of my epigram workshop is a document of about fifty pages. Anything that pops into my mind goes on the first page. If I am driving I stop (really!) and jot it down in the notebook that all writers always have at hand. It doesn't matter how long the thought is; it could be a paragraph. Chances are that the initial thought doesn't work, but often enough it mutates into something with more potential. I try to keep the raw material storeroom under fifty pages, which is around a thousand things I thunk. It's gotten up to 1,500, but that's an unwieldy inventory.

For years I thought that my systematic method was an original contribution—until I discovered Georg Christolph Lichtenberg (1742–1799):

*It is impossible to carry the torch of truth through
a crowd without singeing someone's beard.*

Lichtenberg employed what he called the "waste-book method" of composition, in which he recorded his observations and thoughts, plus anything of interest he heard or read. Which was plenty, because he was a distinguished physicist, mathematician, astronomer, and psychologist.

In the 18th century, merchants recorded every kind of transaction as it occurred in waste-books. Later a clerk would sort out all the kinds of transactions and enter them into a journal. Then a bookkeeper would total each kind and enter them into a ledger. Lichtenberg copied this waste-book-journal-ledger system. I've combined the first two books, because I have a computer, and I can arrange and sort all I want to. But for the epigrammatist, there is nothing new under the sun, including methods of composition.

Each day I work my way through the document. What looks promising advances a few pages, and what is not gets deleted. If an epigram makes it to about page twenty-five it is probably, but not certainly, a keeper. If it makes it to the last page of stage 1, it advances to the appropriate heading in a second document, stage 2, which is the first draft of a book. But making it into the draft is no guarantee of survival. The DELETE button is the most worn key on my keyboard. There is always the clammy dread of producing epigrams that are unclear or just plain stupid. There is also the fear of saying something I heard or read, but forgot that I heard or read. When in doubt I google the epigram every way I can think of, which, predictably leads to many wasted but illuminating hours reading Web sites on long-bows, Stoic philosophy, alchemy, and etiquette.

After much, much rewriting of the draft, I expose my little darlings to some critical readers. I need to be told (ouch!) what doesn't work. It hurts, but it's necessary medicine. Then I work the DELETE button some more, and imagine meeting Boswell and asking him how many stupid things Samuel Johnson said that he left out of *The Life*. Such is the madness in my method—I have a method, but it is hardly methodical. I think of it as mining: first you blast, and then there are big rocks that must be crushed, then screened and sorted into gravel until you find the nuggets and maybe even a diamond.

Let me know what you think. I love to hear from my readers, especially those who have found a use for some-thing I have written—in a seminar, a classroom, a sermon, an anniversary or birthday party, or just to have a way of putting something they already knew into words. Some ask me, "I wrote this. Is it an epigram?" Well, if people are still quoting it in 2,000 years, it probably is.

~:~

A smile is effective at a range of up to thirty feet.

~:~

There are ways of saying yes
that mean no, and of no that mean yes!

~:~

Dignity is never in a rush.

~:~

If a cure were discovered for narcissism,
few would take it.

~:~

It is tragic, but there are people
who are born without a personality.

~:~

~:~

I am annoyed that annoying people are
so untroubled by their annoyingness.

~:~

There are times when you have to get right in
somebody's face, but it works better
if you keep your voice soft.

~:~

You enjoyed listening to a gossip until
you heard what she said about *you*.

~:~

There are two basic personality types: Everything
is a Big Deal and No Big Deal.

~:~

The expression "I am really touched" is a
recognition that touch is something
more powerful than words.

~:~

~:~

After you deliver your parting shot you always
think of one that would have been better.

~:~

Must we thank everyone who played
even the most insignificant role in
making this event possible?

~:~

A party is more interesting if you
talk to the people you don't know.

~:~

Anything you say and do in a rage
is carved in stone.

~:~

~:~

Gossips are like radio stations—
because the things they hear are
first amplified, and then broadcast.

~:~

Surprisingly, there are people who go
through their entire lives without
ever being wrong about anything.

~:~

Making faces is like having the contents
of your brain projected onto a screen.

~:~

Telling stories is no substitute for
holding up your end of a conversation.

~:~

We like to gather in public places where
we can be alone with our computers.

~:~

∼:∼

There is always far more being said
than being heard.

∼:∼

Always keep a lash-length away
from an irritable person.

∼:∼

The three most beautiful words in the
English language are "You were right!"

∼:∼

Someone was rude to you?
So let their rudeness be their problem.

∼:∼

Nothing more infuriating than a
deaf old man pretending to be hearing.

∼:∼

❀:❀

Why would someone answer
the phone saying, "I can't talk now?"

❀:❀

Sometimes the mouth tells one story,
and the rest of the face tells another.

❀:❀

No, I do not want a piece of your mind,
but thanks for the offer.

❀:❀

A good host makes every guest feel special—
if only for a moment.

❀:❀

There are ways in which it is good for
an adult to be childlike, but none in
which it is good to be childish.

❀:❀

~:~

Try not to mistake shyness for unfriendliness.

~:~

If you're a mile wide and an inch deep, you need to
keep changing the subject.

~:~

It's good to be accommodating—
but not good to be a doormat.

~:~

Always trust that small voice in your head
when it says, "Shut up, you idiot!"

~:~

When half the guests have
gone home, be among them.

~:~

~:~

Having a passion for anything
is reason enough to live.

~:~

You wouldn't like to think of yourself
as a discouraging person—
so be an encouraging person!

~:~

Those who need drama in their lives
generally get poor reviews.

~:~

Every day you have only twenty-four hours to live.

~:~

From low self-esteem comes an
insatiable craving for praise.

~:~

~:~

Was it a dull party, or was I the dull party?

~:~

Bad to have all kinds of excuses—
far worse if you believe them.

~:~

When we slip into bitterness we
lose sight of the sweetness of life.

~:~

It only takes one small piece of
good news to make my day.

~:~

Mind your own business very well.

~:~

The different drummer I march
to beats in my heart.

~:~

~:~

The carefree brain has room for
thinking interesting thoughts,
but the worried brain is at capacity.

~:~

Like a worn-out rubber stamp,
some people make almost no impression.

~:~

Real ability is knowing something
to do in almost any situation.

~:~

Unhappiness has always had its devotees.

~:~

I would like to have a button on the dashboard
of my car labeled LAUNCH MISSILE.

~:~

Manipulation fails when you see it as such.

~:~

∾:∾

Tourists complain endlessly,
but real travelers suffer cheerfully.

∾:∾

The neurotic who divides his time
between regretting the past and worrying
about the future has no present at all.

∾:∾

You can only help the willing — the obstinate ones
will create difficulties that will exhaust you.

∾:∾

The magic ingredient of persuasion is a talent for
seeing things from the other person's point of view.

∾:∾

I had a problem with authority when I was young,
and fifty years later I still have one, but it
has become more discriminating.

∾:∾

~:~

Always carry yourself as if your fans are watching.

~:~

You can be funny with people who have no sense
of humor—and you can also get
your head bitten off.

~:~

If you let resentment take root,
it will spring up all over your mind.

~:~

You can make someone happy,
but you can't make someone *be* happy.

~:~

There are times when I am in serious
danger of taking myself seriously.

~:~

~:~

It is dangerous to be alone
in a room with a large pizza.

~:~

There are those who go to the store and select
each cherry, and those who just grab them by the
handful—I'd like to have my cherries selected
by the former, but eat them with the latter.

~:~

The ordering of an 800-calorie dessert must be
preceded by the incantation "I really shouldn't...."

~:~

Chicken is spoken in the kitchens of all nations.

~:~

The adventure of eating cherries is that
each one is a little different from the last.

~:~

FOOD

~:~

It must be strange for a Chinese immigrant to
hear someone saying, "So, you want Chinese?"

~:~

In WASP heaven, the food is
nothing to write home about.

~:~

While we discuss the fine points of poaching
a salmon, elsewhere in the world someone is
cooking a rat on a stick over some burning trash.

~:~

Grabbing a check can be generosity,
or it can be an act of aggression.

~:~

Eat and drink lightly when you need to think—
satiation is the enemy of contemplation.

~:~

∾:∾

Tampering with the recipe for an ethnic dish
that has been perfected over hundreds of years
is like singing a beautiful folk song … off-key.

∾:∾

I love to cook for people who bring good wine
and good conversation—and wash dishes.

∾:∾

The abundance of food we celebrate
on Thanksgiving is our blessing —
and the overabundance is our curse.

∾:∾

When you are a good cook you are frequently
cursed as follows: "You should open a restaurant."

∾:∾

If you want to live a long and healthy life,
keep yourself a little hungry.

∾:∾

∽:∽

Progression is the opposite of progress,
when you're talking about a disease.

∽:∽

Your therapist should know you better
than you know your therapist.

∽:∽

When getting an opinion from a surgeon, keep in
mind that surgeons make their living by cutting.

∽:∽

Our thoughts are a tangled mixture of
reality and unreality—and this stew makes
life interesting and existence bearable.

∽:∽

The benefit of a major health scare is that
it diminishes all your other little worries.

∽:∽

~:~

Dark chocolate or martinis, antidepressants or
ginseng, coffee or chardonnay, aerobics,
television, crosswords or crack cocaine,
we all must have our drugs.

~:~

When you have hay fever the universe
is composed of pollen.

~:~

Skinny people look terrific—with their clothes on.

~:~

If the universe were fair, good-hearted people
would never get heart attacks.

~:~

There is no such a thing as a strong back.

~:~

~:~

My obsessions are my "interests"—
your obsessions are your craziness.

~:~

The doctor gives comfort by sending you home
with a meaningless name for your symptoms.

~:~

Popular medical advice contradicts itself daily.

~:~

No, you haven't lost your mind—
it's rattling around in there somewhere.

~:~

Having a personal trainer is like being a dog.

~:~

You think you've been handling a difficult
situation in your life very well, but then,
suddenly, you are overwhelmed by stress.

~:~

~:~

One of the medical skills is
stating the diagnosis with conviction.

~:~

Drive as if all the other drivers
on the road are drunk.

~:~

You can't argue with an obsession—
but you can humor it.

~:~

Just because you're an adult doesn't mean
you don't need to have a bedtime.

~:~

Hypochondria and quack medicine
are joined at the hip.

~:~

Everyone should be allowed one phobia
without being considered a nut case.

~:~

~:~

The driven will drive six hours
each way to relax for a weekend.

~:~

Shaking hands is an efficient method we
have developed for exchanging our microbes.

~:~

I'm happy with my weight—on the moon.

~:~

You can't know anyone else's mind
if you don't even know your own.

~:~

What makes us crazy differs from person to
person—but there is always something that does.

~:~

~:~

Don't let yourself be rushed
into anything by anybody.

~:~

Every time I lost my way I discovered a new path.

~:~

Don't bother waiting for it all to happen—
it only happens if you make it happen.

~:~

A complicated life is more of a problem for
family and friends than for the person
who causes all the complications.

~:~

You can't live a life that is
both driven and reflective.

~:~

∾∶∾

The more important a person might be
in your life, the more things you
tend to notice about them.

∾∶∾

It's not surprising how much goes wrong,
but how much goes right.

∾∶∾

The average human situation is that things could
be a lot better, but they could also be a lot worse.

∾∶∾

The main problem in philosophy is how to live—
and that is why philosophy is the only field of
study that does not progress.

∾∶∾

The predictable thing about life is that it will be
difficult—the unpredictable thing is how.

∾∶∾

~:~

A new interest can become a new life.

~:~

The purposeful life must struggle with the
constant maddening distractions of everyday life.

~:~

Stupid isn't making a bad mistake in life—
we all do—it's repeating that bad mistake.

~:~

Difficult passages in life are rougher
for those used to smooth sailing.

~:~

Don't try to seem like anything to anybody—
just be your best self.

~:~

Those who prefer to make bad decisions
have little use for good advice.

~:~

∽∶∼

How to live is a more difficult problem
than the origin of the universe.

∽∶∼

Whether you're asking for a job, a date, a favor,
or a loan, desperation is the kiss of death.

∽∶∼

I would like to live in a well-designed life.

∽∶∼

I didn't turn out like they expected—but neither
did I turn out like I expected.

∽∶∼

Many pass their lives simply
waiting for them to be over.

∽∶∼

~:~

This old cloak that I call my skin is mottled
and worn, but I think it will last me.

~:~

Dropping dead is a much more convenient
way to go than the illness method.

~:~

No one can identify the old photo of
the man with the beard, so we toss it, and
that is his last appearance in the world.

~:~

Did you ever arrive somewhere, your mind full of
thoughts, and realize with a start that your
body has been driving for the past hour?

~:~

∻

I wouldn't like to be cremated to
end up in a shoebox in the closet.

∻

The older you get the more
interesting your skin becomes.

∻

In a few years you'll be dust, and you're in
a rage because someone cut in front of you?

∻

Where violence is part of everyday life
it is no deterrent to violence.

∻

If you have a disease that is absolutely fatal,
and you rely on quack medicine,
you are none the worse for it.

∻

∾:∾

Don't try to cheer up someone
who is properly mourning.

∾:∾

Yes, there are some kindly journalists—
they write the obituaries.

∾:∾

When I'm feeling discouraged and I comfort
myself by thinking this too shall pass,
a little voice is saying, "One day it won't."

∾:∾

Longevity is no blessing if you've
always been miserable.

∾:∾

I don't have a minute to spare—
life is calling me, and I have death on hold.

∾:∾

Time

~:~

Just when you get used to being a certain age,
another damn birthday comes along.

~:~

There is an age at which one discovers that
one has a lifetime supply of certain items.

~:~

I love to watch a beautiful sunset—and I have
heard that a sunrise is pretty good too.

~:~

All news is old news, tomorrow.

~:~

Busyness wastes more of life than idleness.

~:~

~:~

The little bit of time we have on earth
is precious—yet we can only relax
by wasting some of it.

~:~

The coins in your pocket are a remnant
of life in the ancient world.

~:~

By the time most people get any money sense,
it's too late for them to get any money.

~:~

I was bored in school because they taught
everything the long way.

~:~

It takes a strong optimist to face
old age cheerfully, but there are many who do.

~:~

~:~

For my grandchildren to know that their grandfather was a hippie is like me knowing that my grandmother was a flapper and that her grandmother was a Bloomer girl.

~:~

We never lack fraudulent reasons for putting off things we should be doing.

~:~

When you get old you will look like an owl— but with large glasses you can look like a wise owl.

~:~

In the dream world everything is at the same time, and everywhere is right next to everywhere else.

~:~

Time is not on anyone's side.

~:~

─────────────────────────────────

~:~

The reason that I am standing here in the garage
is probably that I was going to get something.

~:~

Some people have names that are hard to
remember, and others have faces that are hard
to remember—and a few have names and
faces that are impossible to remember.

~:~

Photos and memories can be
retouched to make them prettier.

~:~

In a desk drawer lie your mystery keys—
you have no idea what they are for, but are
afraid to throw them away, just in case.

~:~

~:~

Everything was amazing when I was little, but
each year it grew a little less so—yet when I recall
my amazement, or see it reflected in the face of
a child, I am again in touch with the absolute
amazingness of everything in this world.

~:~

There is something scary about a friend who
remembers everything you ever said or did.

~:~

Looking back over your life you will discover
that the easiest moments to recall are
first times and last times.

~:~

Memory is a huge cave in which
you have only a tiny candle.

~:~

~:~

When it becomes possible to Google my brain,
I'll stop worrying about Alzheimer's.

~:~

I had a great idea while shaving,
but I forgot it as I rinsed my face.

~:~

The missing part of my brain is called a list—
and I'd better be holding it in my hand
when I get to the store.

~:~

It's reassuring to see other people
looking for their cars in parking lots.

~:~

I pride myself on my memory—
that vast warehouse of trivia.

~:~

∽:∼

The best advice I can give you is
to learn to take good advice.

∽:∼

A pig is much smarter than a pigheaded person.

∽:∼

Are you really sure you know
what it feels like to be an idiot?

∽:∼

We would rather give good advice than take it.

∽:∼

A university is a place in which thought
is neatly compartmentalized.

∽:∼

~:~

An expert is a person who is incapable
of being wrong about a certain subject.

~:~

There is dumb and dumber, but no dumbest.

~:~

Awareness ebbs and flows
as we drift through our day.

~:~

A man of few words might also
be a man of few thoughts.

~:~

Put your helmet on before you start
banging your head on the wall.

~:~

Relying on luck is the plan of many,
but it is not a very good plan.

~:~

∾:∽

Scholarship assumes that the
true facts are always complicated—
common sense assumes that they aren't.

∾:∽

If you don't think you've made a lot of
mistakes in your life, you've learned nothing.

∾:∽

There is a thoughtful place—
located midway between the extremes.

∾:∽

Only call yourself stupid.

∾:∽

Professors talk as if ideas could exist
in the world without context.

∾:∽

The insight can be brilliant without being
completely true in all circumstances.

∾:∽

~:~

A reliable method of simulating wisdom
is cryptic muttering.

~:~

In a very quiet place there is only the
clamor of your thoughts.

~:~

Some textbooks are bound boredom.

~:~

It seemed almost as if one day I was young and
stupid, and the next I was old and wise.

~:~

You can't fit large ideas into small minds.

~:~

It isn't possible to be an angry philosopher.

~:~

~:~

We must raise our consciousness
while lowering our self-consciousness.

~:~

If you consider every aspect of life a problem
to be considered, you might just be a philosopher.

~:~

You can't argue with simple matters of fact,
but people do it all the time.

~:~

The ideal liberal arts education would develop
intellectuals who don't intellectualize.

~:~

When we meet an original thinker
our complacency is shaken.

~:~

Hone your ideas; grind them to a fine edge.

~:~

~:~

I generally get along pretty well
with myself, but I have my moments.

~:~

The enemy of my enemy might be my friend,
but not a friend I would like to
have over for the weekend.

~:~

The meanest man in the world still loves his dog.

~:~

With the gift of being able to see things
through the eyes of others come the
gifts of sympathy and understanding.

~:~

A grudge-master has the art of
cultivating a slight into a major insult.

~:~

~:~

The deeper you go into the thing
that interests you, the smaller the circle
with whom you can discuss it.

~:~

Eventually you learn to make
no firm plans with the flaky.

~:~

A good reason to make new friends is
that your old ones have heard all your stories.

~:~

When your best friends are books they
will always be there for you.

~:~

If getting together with a friend requires
comparing your schedules for the next two
months, your lives are out of control.

~:~

~:~

Always keep an open space
in your life for a new friend.

~:~

When you are young, you talk all night with your
friends about nothing—and it seems profound.

~:~

When you say, "My mind is like that,"
do you mean that you are only
capable of certain thoughts?

~:~

You can sense hostility, even when
it is under lock and key.

~:~

It's surprising how much of a relief
it can be to give up on someone.

~:~

∾:∾

Our society is only the world of people
who include us in their plans.

∾:∾

A funny story about yourself might
be a mean story if it's about a friend.

∾:∾

Try hard to be amusing and you will certainly fail.

∾:∾

You can be most alone in the busiest places.

∾:∾

The shallower your notion of friendship,
the more people you can count as friends.

∾:∾

Choose wisely the people you invite into your
life—and the people you invite out of your life.

∾:∾

~:~

Before you can get something done you
have to know where that thing is.

~:~

The war against clutter is like the war
against terror—it must be unrelenting.

~:~

Clutter is the material expression
of mental disorder.

~:~

It takes a hundred years for a
new neighborhood to become charming.

~:~

Pack rats generally don't miss the
small things you throw away when they
aren't around, as long as you don't go overboard.

~:~

~:~

We live out our lives in just a few
well-worn spots in our homes.

~:~

Growing up in a place that everyone leaves,
your mental bags are always packed.

~:~

The longest job a contractor can get
is remodeling his own home.

~:~

Nature abhors a lawn.

~:~

A bargain on something you didn't
really need is no bargain at all.

~:~

∼:∼

To the extent that you think of your house
as an investment, it is less of a home,
and more of a commodity that you
ought to unload at peak value.

∼:∼

Every tradesman knows that houses can make
otherwise normal people get very crazy.

∼:∼

A bad neighborhood is one
in which the intolerable is tolerated.

∼:∼

Teenagers raised in endless subdivisions and
shopping malls laced together by freeways
understand alienation without knowing the word.

∼:∼

When you are deep in thought is not a good time
to be washing the best china.

∼:∼

∾:∾

You don't get what you need by being needy.

∾:∾

Online dating would work better
if a method were discovered for
piping pheromones over the Internet.

∾:∾

Many a bad argument could
have been averted with a hug.

∾:∾

If your parents really loved you, you always feel
you are a worthwhile person, no matter what
happens in life.

∾:∾

To study first-date behaviors,
go to an art museum.

∾:∾

~:~

We should have fifty words for
the different kinds of love.

~:~

Let a love affair that is over be over—remember
the good times, but don't look back, don't replay,
don't try to understand, don't look for lessons,
and don't regret anything.

~:~

We know what attracts us, but haven't a clue
why we find such a person so attractive.

~:~

If only we spent as much time caressing
each other as we do our keyboards.

~:~

First there is the silent question:
"If I ask you for a date will you say yes?"

~:~

~:~

Freedom—the enemy of commitment.

~:~

If you turn into the Spanish Inquisition
on the first date, you probably won't get a second.

~:~

The man who is very good at romance
is often not very good at relationships.

~:~

Sexiness is a declining asset that still produces a
high rate of interest until it is fully depreciated.

~:~

The only treasures we really
have to give are love and kindness.

~:~

A singles event is a roomful of
people who haven't lost all hope.

~:~

~:~

Girls know instinctively how to flirt—
but boys must be taught how to be romantic.

~:~

A morning person and a night person—
it will never work.

~:~

The people browsing the relationship section
of a bookstore may not be very good at
relationships — but they're working on it.

~:~

First loves are full of misunderstandings.

~:~

When you feel sexy, you are.

~:~

~:~

The problem for would-be matchmakers is that
while common interests are easy to find,
attraction remains the great mystery.

~:~

Teenage girls converse at the speed of light.

~:~

The smartest and the dumbest kids
get into trouble, but the smart ones
pass through the trouble.

~:~

Your early years were a series
of experiments in managing adults.

~:~

Does a man finally understand
women after his sex change?

~:~

~:~

They kept their unhappy marriage
together for the sake of the children—
because that's what their parents did.

~:~

Seated at the farthest table with the distant
cousins and the ex-neighbors, you feel
like you barely made the cut.

~:~

You know how to push buttons in your family—
and what happens when you do—
so why do you keep pushing those buttons?

~:~

The art of listening should be taught
in all schools, because few will learn it at home.

~:~

I'll just keep saying it until you
get tired of not hearing it.

~:~

~:~

You can do a lot of leaving in your life—
but all your baggage follows.

~:~

Lacking the ability to express our feelings,
we validate certain occasions by
spending a lot of money.

~:~

If your little boy is never bad, you should seek
professional help as soon as possible.

~:~

In a flash, rage transforms beauty
into a hideous mask.

~:~

Two poor listeners can be happy together,
as neither expects to be heard.

~:~

~:~

Placing all your hopes on
your children is a very risky bet.

~:~

If you have any sense, your concept
of what is sexy ages as you do.

~:~

A family has a way of simply forgetting the
existence of a difficult and angry relative.

~:~

We do not practice equal opportunity forgiveness.

~:~

Dysfunctional is repeating behavior
that didn't work the first time.

~:~

There are people whose lives are ruined
if they never have children, and others
whose lives are ruined if they do.

~:~

~:~

A common misconception is that
your family is crazier than most.

~:~

Not honoring your parents is
dishonoring yourself.

~:~

Unconditional love from your parents
is a very good start in life, but few
are lucky enough to get it.

~:~

It is the egg that chooses the sperm, and takes her
time about it—and this is how men learn to wait.

~:~

Parents don't like their parents
telling them how to parent.

~:~

~:~

Western acting is as stylized
as the Noh theater of Japan—
we're just used to the conventions.

~:~

Things turn out well in light opera
and badly in heavy opera.

~:~

You can't write about things that can't be
put into words—but poets never stop trying.

~:~

Spam writers are the first authors
to use the entire keyboard.

~:~

Originality is the sauce that makes
familiar things interesting.

~:~

~:~

No one loves words more than a two-year-old
who is just learning what they mean.

~:~

Good to have a large vocabulary,
but even better to use it sparingly.

~:~

Acclaim may be gratifying to an artist,
but it cuts into studio time.

~:~

A playwright often runs out of ideas
in the middle of the second act.

~:~

Some commas are just a place to rest for a spell,
on your trek through the sentence.

~:~

Writer's block can generally be cured by writing.

~:~

~:~

The raw material of art is life, just as wine
is made from sun, dirt, and water.

~:~

Your first creative act, on the wall
with a crayon, was greeted with horror.

~:~

You could fill the Hollywood Bowl
with forgotten stars.

~:~

When the fine arts become as creative
as advertising, we will be living
in another Renaissance.

~:~

The collector gets more pleasure
from the painting than the artist does,
because the artist sees only an attempt.

~:~

~:~

An angry poet can write nothing but doggerel.

~:~

Write in your true voice, and you will be heard.

~:~

When you discover the thing that really interests
you, other interests begin to drop away.

~:~

The voices of my angels offer encouragement—
but my demons drive me to do my best work.

~:~

Keep a copy of this book in your pocket in case
you should have to make an impromptu speech,
or be stuck in an elevator for six hours.

~:~

By reading the classics we learn that
everything has already been said.

~:~

~:~

When acting is good, we are no longer
in the audience, we are in the play.

~:~

Faked originality is grotesque.

~:~

I keep changing the sentence until I get it right—
and in that moment I hear something
click into place.

~:~

As long as I confine my madness to my art,
I'm no danger to myself, only to society.

~:~

All writing filled with jargon
will soon be forgotten.

~:~

These words that I write are only
souvenirs of my mind's adventures.

~:~

∼:∼

You may ask what is the right thing to do,
but in your heart you already know.

∼:∼

Moral authority is the hardest kind
of authority to acquire.

∼:∼

Never tell someone at a reunion that they must
remember you—because that forces them
to pretend they do.

∼:∼

The main opportunities for people of poor
character come from finding people
who are poor judges of character.

∼:∼

Avoid people who are always right—
unless you enjoy always being wrong.

∼:∼

❦

The finger of blame points
outward in all directions.

❦

We flaunt our little sins, like a weakness for
sweets, and keep the big ones to ourselves.

❦

Nature gives children personalities;
parents give them values.

❦

That your great-great grandfather
was a horse thief is amusing—
that your father was an embezzler is not.

❦

We go through life hearing few lies—
but plenty of the truth being bent, filtered,
retouched, twisted, shaded, and massaged.

❦

~:~

The mentality of criminals is
so contagious it infects even the police.

~:~

You have only to be caught in a single lie
to become known as a liar.

~:~

Half of police work is a stupid treasure hunt
for bags of useless powders and weeds.

~:~

You should devote ten seconds a day to
worrying about what other people will think.

~:~

Charisma blinds our eyes to the
completely fraudulent.

~:~

∾:∿

Human nature is, for most purposes, only the
nature of the people you allow into your life.

∾:∿

The most effective truth serum is 80 proof.

∾:∿

Having to reply to an uncomfortable question
doesn't mean that you have to reply to *that
particular* uncomfortable question.

∾:∿

A martyr is someone who throws his
life away for something you believe in.

∾:∿

The simple truth is the only kind there is.

∾:∿

Vanity

∼:∼

You can't make up stories for
the people who read you like a book.

∼:∼

The most useful volunteers
will do anything except serve on a board.

∼:∼

Men will notice a short skirt more
than a tastefully chosen outfit.

∼:∼

We score some cheap easy virtue by
giving change to a homeless person, recycling
a little plastic pill bottle, or doing a few
minutes of halfhearted exercise.

∼:∼

A movie-star-quality facelift is
so good it almost fools you.

∼:∼

∾⦂∾

If you had to write down ten totally honest
statements describing your personality, would
you be willing to share them with anyone?

∾⦂∾

Money and sex—the bricks and mortar
of our fantasy lives.

∾⦂∾

A "good editorial" is one that states
the opinion we already held.

∾⦂∾

We are all the stars of our own reality shows.

∾⦂∾

My opinion of myself reaches a low when I
bite my tongue severely while eating a sandwich.

∾⦂∾

~:~

Young people must pose because
they don't know what they are yet.

~:~

The flunky must prove his status by
being more arrogant than the master.

~:~

Better to remain unknown than
to have once been famous.

~:~

If you have a fear of being boring,
just keep people talking about themselves.

~:~

The great talent of a narcissist is a knack for
turning any subject, no matter how unrelated,
into something about himself.

~:~

❧

If our egos were our skins there would
be scars on the scar tissue.

❧

The one place we do not enjoy seeing
our reflection is in the pupils of our dentist.

❧

Ask a few leading questions and
most people will tell you everything.

❧

We prefer the natural over the artificial,
except when the natural is unflattering.

❧

There's nothing wrong with being eccentric if
you're an English lord with plenty of money—
otherwise, you should keep it under control.

❧

∼:∼

Better to get up and dance badly than
to sit and watch the dancing.

∼:∼

I'm planning to enter a liar's contest
and tell this short, but sure-fire winner:
"I have absolutely no regrets in my life."

∼:∼

We prefer to believe that others think well of
us, because the alternative is too unpleasant to
consider.

∼:∼

How strange that a few hundred years ago
men displayed their legs in silk stockings
while women concealed theirs...

∼:∼

~:~

It's easy to stay current—all you have to do
is read twenty-four hours a day.

~:~

California is always also a state of mind.

~:~

To a farmer, a close neighbor is a mile away;
to a city apartment dweller, a neighbor snoring
on the other side of the bedroom wall.

~:~

Entering a new culture is like having to fit
a second skin on top of your old one.

~:~

There is someone interesting living on any
block of any street anywhere in the world.

~:~

~:~

Young people will travel halfway around the world
to sit in a bar with other young tourists.

~:~

We Americans are mongrels, always eager to start
yapping about the ethnicity of our ancestors.

~:~

The mind of an intellectual is poisoned
by even a tinge of bigotry.

~:~

Americans do not save because in our culture
we gain more status from consumption.

~:~

When traveling we are refreshed
by the differentness of things.

~:~

~:~

This work of civilization has barely begun.

~:~

An American conversation: "I'm Polish."
"So when did you come here?" "Well, actually
my grandparents came here in 1920."

~:~

There is nothing the city offers
that is compensation for never
seeing a sky filled with stars.

~:~

There are countries where we are loved
and countries where we are hated—
but trying to resist the onslaught of American
culture would be like trying to repel the weather.

~:~

Thanks to the grinding poverty of the natives,
our vacation was a terrific bargain!

~:~

~:~

We have no problem with illegal immigrants
ministering to many of our needs—
the problem is having to minister
to some of theirs.

~:~

The observer of society must always
be standing a little apart.

~:~

There are a thousand different
"real Americas"—each as real as the next.

~:~

When people of two very different
cultures meet, they often share a feeling
that the other is very backward.

~:~

∽:∽

I would cast plenty of stones,
if only I were without sin.

∽:∽

There is no limit to the
spiritual wealth you can acquire.

∽:∽

Leviticus is no fun.

∽:∽

Globalization is bad news for local gods.

∽:∽

There is often a moment in a sermon when
the preacher looks like he's not sure where
he is going with what he is saying.

∽:∽

∾:∾

God chuckles at ten seconds of blasphemy
when you whack your thumb with a hammer.

∾:∾

At a silent retreat I discovered
that I really didn't have much to say.

∾:∾

Fundamentalists and scientists agree that
the world is coming to an end, their only
difference being seven billion years.

∾:∾

Religion is a marketplace of wisdom and values,
and only what is useful deserves to survive.

∾:∾

Step one of becoming a guru is
downloading a lot of wisdom.

∾:∾

~:~

If there were no organized religions
we could all be one religion.

~:~

A religion may be ecumenical,
but it does not like to share its followers.

~:~

The miracle is that I'm as
religious as I am, considering the atheism.

~:~

Behave as if the fly on the wall were God.

~:~

God created man in His image—then He got
really busy and created 950,000 species of insects.

~:~

Religion will outlast any belief in the supernatural.

~:~

~:~

A government that is not feared could not
collect enough taxes to make a living for itself.

~:~

Absolute certainty is the privilege of fanatics.

~:~

A well-regulated militia would not
enlist paranoid gun nuts.

~:~

Politicians are the hand puppets
of their speechwriters.

~:~

A three-year-old snatches a toy from his playmate,
and this is the beginning of imperialism.

~:~

~:~

It takes a lot of money getting elected to
the Senate, but there is even more
money in being an ex-senator.

~:~

Because we find people more interesting
than ideas or events, we can hardly blame the
media for a shallow focus on personalities.

~:~

The price of freedom is blood, but not
the blood of those who arranged the transaction.

~:~

What normal person would seek high office?

~:~

When charisma enters the room,
common sense goes out the window.

~:~

~:~

A white person has no defense against
a charge of unconscious racism.

~:~

A political party does the least
for a constituency it has in its pocket.

~:~

Fervently believing that you're a
victim of injustice is about the same
as actually being a victim of injustice.

~:~

It is unfair that polls influence elections,
even when they're wrong.

~:~

Can you tell where the news ends
and the propaganda begins?

~:~

~:~

When the presidential couple go to bed,
a Secret Service agent is always stationed at
their bedroom door—not listening, of course.

~:~

In the military you learn how to follow orders
exactly, including those that will make you dead.

~:~

As their cities were being leveled,
the Germans began to grasp the
fundamental errors of Nazi thought.

~:~

In the perfect bureaucracy,
the buck stops nowhere.

~:~

The oppressed peoples of the world long for
democracy—but not for our kind of democracy.

~:~

~:~

The minority cannot but feel wronged
when the majority is an ass.

~:~

A public figure with even half a brain says
absolutely nothing "off the record."

~:~

We go to war to preserve our way of life—
a way of life featuring a strong military
and a readiness to go to war.

~:~

The basic idea of an army is that you can
kill people without murdering them.

~:~

The intelligence of a government that both admits
and justifies torture is somewhat open to question.

~:~

~:~

One more word about conspiracies
and you're on my list of airheads.

~:~

Extremists think in historical terms more than
most people—but only to confirm their prejudices.

~:~

The leftist has chosen a marginal life on the
fringes of society, and viewing society from that
fringe, he produces a cockeyed critique of it.

~:~

Protest demonstrations validate the importance of
their leaders—by proving that they have followers.

~:~

~:~

It was awkward learning to stand on our hind legs,
but after only two million years, we are able to
operate computers with our front paws.

~:~

A wilderness trail is a freeway for backpackers,
loaded like pack mules with granola and gadgets.

~:~

We are an invasive species.

~:~

Accepting an invitation for a sail is like
going to a party that you aren't allowed
to leave until the host decides it's over.

~:~

In California we expect nature to
periodically kick our butts.

~:~

~:~

It is impossible to swim in the ocean
without thinking of *Jaws.*

~:~

From the viewpoint of a fly,
a human is most useful when dead.

~:~

As a bird hunts twigs for her nest,
so we head for the home center.

~:~

Four tons of automobiles in your driveway,
and you talk about the environment?

~:~

Once, we all got everything we needed by crying.

~:~

~:~

The art of camping is making do
without what you forgot to bring.

~:~

Your dog is not adorable if it's in the habit
of sticking its nose in people's crotches.

~:~

Nature always finds ways to
limit a population—as it will our own.

~:~

Birds teach us to keep our eyes open.

~:~

The stoic character supposedly created
by harsh winters is actually a symptom
of seasonal depression.

~:~

A garden is a state of unnatural nature.

~:~

~:~

Farming is a partnership between man and nature
in which nature is the majority partner.

~:~

The landscape of your childhood is
the one that is most real to you.

~:~

Naturally, I tried hard to be natural,
but it's not my nature.

~:~

Watching my fingers moving over this
keyboard, they resemble the legs
of a crab roaming the sea floor.

~:~

Bird watchers and hunters occasionally meet in
the woods, but they have little to talk about.

~:~

~:~

We share ninety-seven percent of our genes with
chimpanzees—I treasure the other three percent.

~:~

Never rule out the highly improbable; it is
possible, for example, that a very tall woman in
high heels in a gay bar is actually a woman.

~:~

The lands of the world are mostly empty,
because humans tend to swarm.

~:~

We are constantly seeking explanations,
but many things are the way they are
for no particular reason.

~:~

In ideas, size matters.

~:~

~:~

Densely written jargon is a method
scholars use to disguise a lack of content.

~:~

The best arguments against the theory
of evolution are the brains of the
fundamentalists who reject it.

~:~

Due to Heisenberg's uncertainty principle,
a small object, when dropped, will roll farther
away than seems possible and then disappear.

~:~

Regarding all of humanity's future plans, all bets
are off due to the randomness of the universe.

~:~

If you are a mosquito, the great mystery
of the universe is mosquito repellent.

~:~

∾∶∾

We know that we don't understand the science
behind the computer on our desk, but actually
we don't even understand the desk.

∾∶∾

From the viewpoint of a virus that lives twenty
minutes, we are almost immortal,
yet the virus can kill us.

∾∶∾

Science is an idea that married a grant
and gave birth to a discovery.

∾∶∾

Taking everything into consideration—
it would be impossible to ever make a decision.

∾∶∾

The word "proven" belongs more
to marketing than to science.

∾∶∾

—————————————————

~:~

Technology is burying us in new features.

~:~

I had a nightmare in which my life was ruined
because I had forgotten all my passwords.

~:~

Assembly instructions are written by gremlins.

~:~

The difference between a brilliant inventor
and a brilliant crackpot is the filter.

~:~

As technology continues to reduce our attention
span from minutes to seconds to fractions of a
second, it becomes difficult to communicate any
thought that cannot be grasped in a few words.

~:~

~:~

The command on your computer
that could destroy your life is called *send*.

~:~

We Americans have an advantage in technology
because in many countries an educated person
would never touch a tool.

~:~

Information junkies are beginning
to die from overdoses.

~:~

The word "repair" has been
replaced by the word "replace."

~:~

They laugh in the face of gravity—
those engineers of skyscrapers,
bridges, and brassieres.

~:~

~:~

Science and technology are at work
against democracy as they deliver increasingly
sophisticated means of manipulating
a confused electorate.

~:~

Just you and me—and the phone, our cell phones,
radio, TV, Internet, and the thousand
things that are on our minds.

~:~

The ultimate thing to be feared from technology
is a time when thoughts are no longer private.

~:~

Walking into a lamp post while texting
is an instant message from reality.

~:~

The Internet allows you to have the illusion
that by interacting, you are acting.

~:~

Work

~:~

From den mother to big brother, from docent to
volunteering at an animal shelter, the best jobs you
can ever have pay absolutely nothing.

~:~

Just try, in your life, to do one thing
really, really well.

~:~

Creative excuses show imagination—but those
who offer them were seldom hired
for their imagination.

~:~

There are times when you must ignore everyone
around you if you are to get anything done—but
these situations only occur about twice a day.

~:~

❧

Retirement is sad when your work is your life—
but a joy when your life is your work.

❧

A good salesman is a chameleon with
rhinoceros hide and the persistence
of a mosquito in your bedroom at night.

❧

A boring career finds its consolation
in extreme recreation.

❧

Among the many advantages of being extremely
busy are having less work assigned to you,
seeming more important than you are,
and always having a ready excuse.

❧

The perfect waiter is attentive, accommodating,
informative—and just a touch subservient.

❧

~:~

Students will always love a teacher
who is in love with teaching.

~:~

The workaholic fears not
being missed when he's on vacation.

~:~

"I hear you" is a nice way of dodging the issue.

~:~

The longest question directed at a speaker
invariably contains no question at all.

~:~

Those who expect to live dull lives
after college tend to party hardest.

~:~

When the boss is nuts
the office becomes an asylum.

~:~

~:~

Always respect that people who do menial work
must try to preserve their dignity in small ways.

~:~

Natural leaders are not created
in leadership training seminars.

~:~

Interesting work is a
bargain over boring work,
even at half the pay.

~:~

Many consultants are rarely consulted.

~:~

Productivity increases because ten percent of the
employees are willing to do the additional work
assigned to the other ninety percent.

~:~

∾:∾

When someone asks you what you do,
you could say, "Do about what?"

∾:∾

"I was multitasking"—that's what
type A personalities say when
they've messed up their work.

∾:∾

Better to have had a career as a good worker
than as a terrible boss.

∾:∾

Ambition is a race in which you
are permitted to make many false starts.

∾:∾

Most people will never know
anything better than a job.

∾:∾

❦

There are tasks we never get to because
they're too exhausting even to think about.

❦

You can make your point without
throwing in the history of the world.

❦

Talking often impersonates teaching.

❦

You imagined that a workaholic would be
productive, until you had one working for you.

❦

There are jobs that are very stressful—
and then there are the people
who find any job very stressful.

❦

~:~

Employees are not slaves—because they
have the right to change masters.

~:~

There's nothing wrong with
entering a career through a backdoor—
but you had better be a fast learner.

~:~

Every interruption adds twice
its length to the task.

~:~

Necessity is also the mother of shoddy things
thrown together at the last minute.

~:~

I'd rather hire a carpenter who writes poetry
than a poet who does carpentry.

~:~

~:~

To survive in a corporate office you must
either be doing something useful, or appear
to be doing something useful.

~:~

The favor bank is always open for new deposits.

~:~

You can tell when you are nearing the center of
power, because the suits are better fitting.

~:~

Ten seconds of thought could have
prevented a year of damage control.

~:~

Capitalism is always thinking of ways
to eliminate the small operator.

~:~

∻

The enormous advertising industry is
an inverted pyramid resting on the
shaky premise that advertising works.

∻

The business traveler pretends to work, as if to
deny that so much of his life is being wasted.

∻

If your word is your bond, it is reasonable
for it to carry a very high interest rate.

∻

There would be no stock market if the bulls
weren't right a little more often than the bears.

∻

The stock market smiles on a company that
dumps thousands of well-paid older workers,
most of whom will never again have decent
jobs — because the market has no heart.

∻

∼:∼

It's the sure things that turn out really badly.

∼:∼

As the general can lose a battle but not his command, so the executive can make a decision that costs thousands of people their jobs and not lose his own.

∼:∼

When Asia discovers individuality, they will bury us.

∼:∼

The only subject that endlessly fascinates the media is the media.

∼:∼

They can make the employees say, "Thank you sir, have a nice day." But they can't make them add inflection, emphasis, or eye contact.

∼:∼

∼:∼

A contradiction of capitalism is that
it depends on both saving and spending.

∼:∼

Easy credit in our materialistic society
has reduced many to a state of bondage
enforced by the laws of the nation.

∼:∼

For every billionaire there are a thousand
millionaires, and for every millionaire
there are a thousand thousandaires.

∼:∼

When the economy crashes, you need to keep
your head, even if you've lost everything else.

∼:∼

The mark of an amateur investor
is believing in a stock.

∼:∼

~:~

What you own lets you sleep—
what you owe keeps you up at night.

~:~

He bragged about the stock that doubled,
but forgot to mention the one that halved.

~:~

The rise and fall of the economy is a
force of nature that central bankers
and economists pretend to manage.

~:~

If you have money at the end of a business career,
you are never really sure if it is due to your skill
and wisdom, or to the dumb luck of having
been in the right place at the right time.

~:~

When investors get greedy, that is
when the serious money is lost.

~:~

~:~

I wish I had a dollar for every dollar I ever had.

~:~

Economies worked well enough
before there were economists.

~:~

In the locker room you hear smart opinions
about sports and dumb ones about investments.

~:~

When we say that they have money, or that they
don't have money, we are really saying that they
have more or less money than we have.

~:~

A nation of debtors is not a free people.

~:~

Alchemy didn't disappear, it was
transmuted into economics.

~:~

~:~

MICHAEL LIPSEY lives in San Rafael, California, and divides his time between writing and artwork. He loves to hear from his readers, especially those who have put his epigrams to work. If you have enjoyed this book, why not take a look at the first in the series, titled *I Thought So — A Book of Epigrams.*

And watch for the gestating third and final (perhaps) book of the series, in which all the great questions of mankind will be raised, and left hanging there, unanswered. Answers, you can get for free on the Internet — as many as you want, more than you need. Epigrams are questions about the answers, and questions about the questions. We ask the questions not to get answers, but to share what we have learned about how to live.

~:~

The epigram Web site is **www.ithoughtso.net**
E-mail: **mike@ithoughtso.net**

Index

Bold *entries indicate chapter themes.*